AQUILAS K DAPAAH

ARISE
DEBORAH ACTIVATION

60 Days to Arise in Faith, Leadership & Purpose

WORBOOK

*A Companion Devotional to the book:
Arise, As the Deborah You Are Called to Be.*

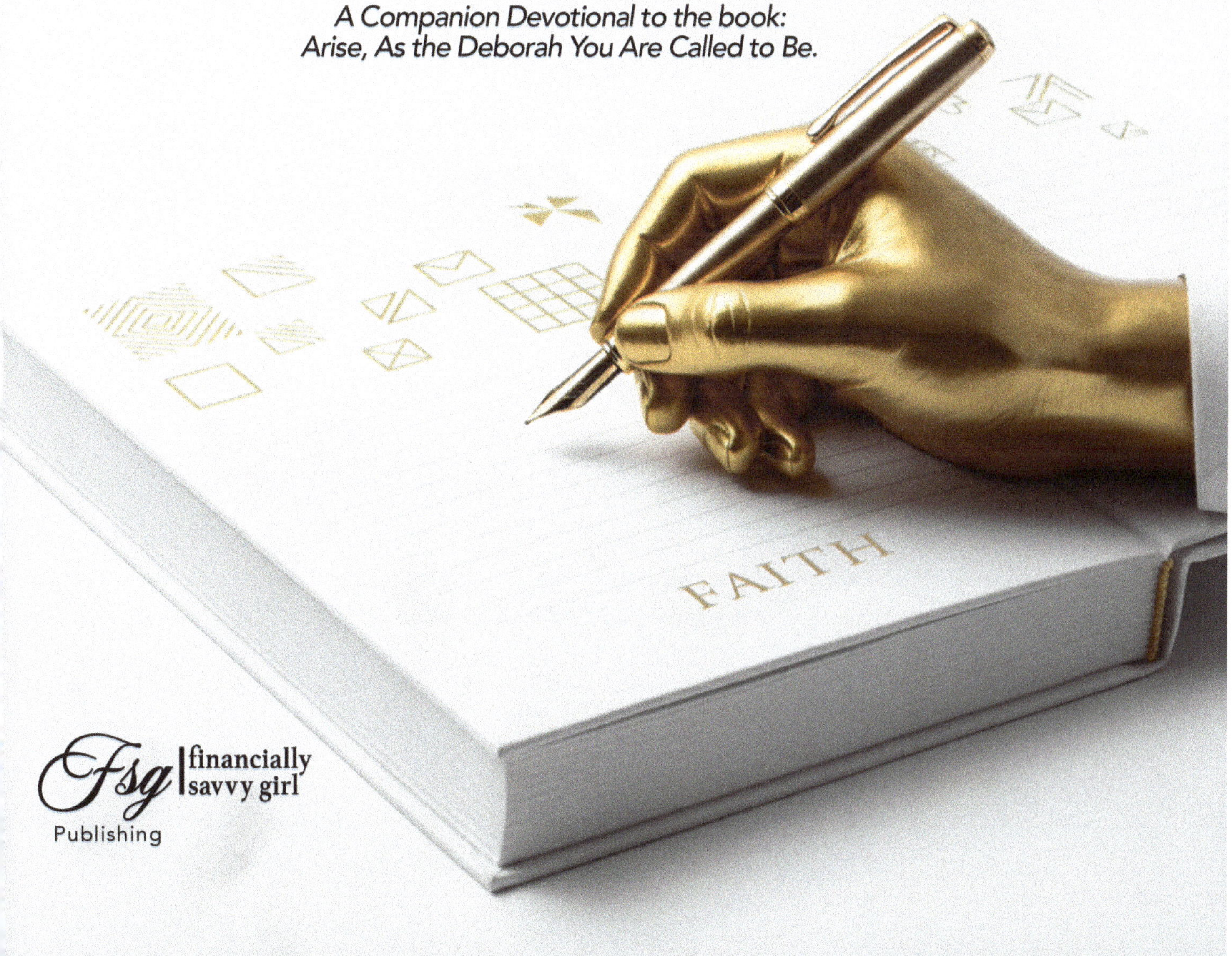

Fsg | financially savvy girl
Publishing

THE DEBORAH ACTIVATION

WORKBOOK

60 DAYS TO ARISE IN FAITH, LEADERSHIP & PURPOSE

By Aquilas K Dapaah

A Companion Devotional to the book:
Arise, As the Deborah You Are Called to Be.

Published by FSG Publishing,
Editorial Imprint of Financially Savvy Girl Inc

This devotional belongs to:

_____

This workbook is the continuation and activation of your Deborah journey, the practical companion to the book Arise, As the Deborah You Are Called to Be. Over the next 60 days, you will move from revelation to action, deepening your faith, sharpening your leadership and aligning your purpose with God's call on your life.

It is designed to awaken and strengthen the Deborah within you: bold in faith, wise in leadership and steadfast in purpose.

Step into each day ready to arise, apply, and activate the Deborah within you.

© 2025 Financially Savvy Girl Inc.

All rights reserved.

No portion of this workbook may be reproduced, stored in a retrieval system, or transmitted in any form or by any means—electronic, mechanical, photocopying, recording, or otherwise—without prior written permission from the publisher, except for brief quotations used in reviews or scholarly work.

Scripture quotations are taken from the Holy Bible, New Living Translation (NLT). Copyright © Tyndale House Foundation. Used by permission.

Published by FSG Publishing, editorial

Imprint of Financially Savvy Girl Inc.

www.financiallysavvygirl.com

DEDICATION

To every woman who has felt the nudge of purpose pulling her forward...

This workbook was written to accompany you as you rise.

May these pages guide your steps, strengthen your resolve and deepen your faith as you walk out the lessons in the book Arise, As the Deborah You Are Called to Be.

This is your season to move with clarity, courage and conviction.

May your journey lead others to rise because you chose to.

FOREWORD

When I wrote Arise, As the Deborah You Are Called to Be, my prayer was that it would awaken something powerful within you, a stirring, a holy courage, a steady clarity about who God called you to be. I believed it would ignite a generation of women rising in wisdom, excellence and unshakeable faith.

But I also knew something essential:

inspiration without activation eventually fades.

Revelation must meet discipline.

Faith must meet strategy.

Identity must meet implementation.

That is why I created The Deborah Activation Workbook.

There is a sound rising in this generation, a sound of women awakening to purpose, authority, and divine wisdom. We live in a world that glorifies speed, applause, and visibility, yet Heaven is calling us to something deeper: discernment, devotion and depth. The world does not need louder voices; it needs truer ones.

This devotional-workbook is more than a companion to Arise;

it is the continuation of your Deborah journey,

the bridge between what God revealed to you and the woman you are becoming, day by day.

In these 60 days, you will learn to apply the principles of Arise in the rhythms of your real life:

in your home, your leadership, your business, your finances, your relationships, your spiritual walk and your calling.

You will not simply study Deborah's story,

you will step into it.

You will learn to lead with clarity, to hear God before you move, to walk in courage even when you feel unqualified and to live with the excellence, strategy and faith required for your assignment.

As you journey, let this be more than reading.

Let it become a rhythm…

prayer, reflection, action, alignment and transformation.

Take your time. Go deep.

Do not rush the work God desires to unfold within you.

Let every page remind you that leadership begins in stillness, that courage grows through obedience and that your influence is never accidental, it is Heaven's assignment.

The Deborah generation is rising.

And you are part of it.

> *"Arise, shine, for your light has come, and the glory of the Lord rises upon you."* — Isaiah 60:1 (NLT)

Aquilas K. Dapaah

NOTE TO THE READER

This workbook is a sacred space for reflection and transformation.

Approach it slowly. Allow each day to speak to you with clarity and intention.

There will be entries that comfort, and others that stretch you.

Both are necessary. Growth requires honesty, time, and the willingness to listen deeply.

Write freely in the lined pages that follow each devotional.

Your notes—whether clear or unfinished—are part of your spiritual formation.

Remember: this journey is not about acquiring information.

It is about becoming the woman God has called you to be.

INTRODUCTION

You are not here by accident.

There is a divine calling over your life, one that requires clarity, courage, faith and action. Like Deborah, you have been chosen to lead, to rise and to step into the fullness of your God-given purpose. But walking in that calling takes more than a moment of inspiration; it requires daily alignment with God's voice and a willingness to be formed from the inside out.

That is why this workbook was created.

The Deborah Activation Workbook: 60 Days to Arise in Faith, Leadership & Purpose is the continuation of your Deborah journey - the bridge between revelation and transformation.
The book Arise, As the Deborah You Are Called to Be plants the vision; this workbook helps you live it. It was designed to help you walk out the principles of Arise not in theory, but in practice: in your home, your leadership, your business, your finances, your relationships and your spiritual life.

Over the next 60 days, you will move intentionally from understanding to implementation. Each day will guide you through Scripture, reflection, prayer and a practical activation step. At the end of every week, you'll also find a "Mentor Moment": a focused coaching style reflection to sharpen your hinking and stretch your leadership and then followed end of each week with a "Deborah Activation Journal" : a space to pause, assess, realign, and capture what God is shaping within you. This is not just about what you read; it is about who you are becoming.

This workbook is a sacred space for reflection and transformation. Approach it slowly. Allow each day to speak to you with clarity and intention. There will be entries that comfort you and others that stretch you. Both are necessary. Growth requires honesty, time and the willingness to listen deeply.

Write freely in the pages that follow each devotional page and week. your notes, whether clear or unfinished, are part of your spiritual formation. Do not rush your process. Even if you miss a day, return with grace. This is not about perfection; it is about progress, alignment and obedience.

Remember: this journey is not about acquiring information.

It is about becoming the woman God has called you to be:

a Deborah in this generation: bold in faith, wise in leadership, and steadfast in purpose.

As you move through these pages, come with expectancy. Let each day build on the last. Let each step draw you deeper into the call that already rests on your life.

Arise, and walk it out.

With love,

Aqui

HOW TO USE THIS DEVOTIONAL

A 60-Day Leadership Activation Journey

This devotional is designed to guide you through 60 days of intentional transformation.

Every entry is crafted to strengthen your faith, refine your leadership, and activate your God-given purpose, one day at a time.

This is not a journey to be rushed.

Go slow. Go deep. Let each day's message work in you.

1. Set the Atmosphere

Choose a consistent time and space to meet with God daily.

Bring your Bible, this devotional, and a journal.

Begin each session by inviting the Holy Spirit to speak to you.

This time is sacred, guard it.

2. Follow the Daily Flow

Every devotional entry follows a simple but powerful rhythm:

- Scripture (NLT): Read slowly. Let the Word minister to you.

- Reflection: Allow the message to speak to your leadership, character, and purpose.

- Prayer: Begin with the written prayer, then continue in your own words.

- Action Step: Apply what you've read through intentional, practical movement.

Do not rush through the process.

Some days will invite stillness; others will stir bold action.

Both are necessary for your growth.

3. Embrace the Weekly Rhythm

At the end of each week, you'll find a Deborah Activation Journal, which includes:

- Heart Alignment: What God is shaping within you

- Leadership in Motion: How you're being stretched as a leader

- Business & Strategy Activation: Applying spiritual wisdom to practical work

- Kingdom in Motion Challenge: A weekly assignment that advances your purpose

If you're walking through this journey with others, this journal becomes a powerful tool for accountability and group reflection.

4. Read with an Open Heart and a Ready Hand

Approach each day with expectation.

Highlight what resonates.

Revisit what convicts or comforts you.

Transformation happens through repetition, reflection, and response, not speed.

5. Mark Your Milestones

Every ten days, pause and look at how you've evolved.

Celebrate the shifts in your mindset, habits, confidence, and spiritual sensitivity.

These moments are evidence of God at work in you.

6. Prepare for Multiplication

This devotional is not only about your personal transformation, it's about your assignment.

As God strengthens you, ask:

Who am I being prepared to lead, mentor, or influence?

Deborah's calling was not individual; it was generational. Yours is too.

Remember This

You are not just reading…

you are rising.

Take this devotional one day at a time, with grace and intention.

The goal is depth, not speed.

Formation, not completion.

The Holy Spirit will meet you on every page.

TABLE OF CONTENTS

Copyright Page
Dedication
Foreword
Note to the Reader
Introduction
How to Use This Devotional

PART I — THE JOURNEY BEGINS

Week 1 — Answering the Call
- Day 1: You Are Called
- Day 2: Chosen for a Purpose
- Day 3: Overcoming Fear
- Day 4: Walking by Faith
- Day 5: A Willing Heart
- Day 6: Strength for the Journey
- Day 7: Preparing for the Next Step
- Mentor Moment — Week 1
- Deborah Activation Journal — Week 1

Week 2 — Courage in Leadership
- Day 8: The Call to Lead
- Day 9: The Power of Obedience
- Day 10: Courage in Conflict
- Day 11: Speaking with Authority
- Day 12: Leading with Compassion
- Day 13: Wisdom in Decision Making
- Day 14: Trusting God's Timing
- Mentor Moment — Week 2
- Deborah Activation Journal — Week 2

Week 3 — **Boldness in Action**
- Day 15: Stepping Forward in Faith
- Day 16: The Discipline of Consistency
- Day 17: Breaking Limiting Beliefs
- Day 18: Taking Initiative
- Day 19: The Strength to Stand Alone
- Day 20: Faith That Builds Momentum
- Day 21: Finishing What You Start
- Mentor Moment — Week 3
- Deborah Activation Journal — Week 3

Week 4 — **Wisdom and Strategy**
- Day 22: The Wisdom to Wait and Listen
- Day 23: Strategy from the Spirit
- Day 24: The Counsel of Many
- Day 25: The Power of Vision
- Day 26: Strategy in Stewardship
- Day 27: Strategic Partnerships
- Day 28: Executing with Excellence
- Mentor Moment — Week 4
- Deborah Activation Journal — Week 4

PART II — THE DEBORAH WITHIN

Week 5 — **Godly Leadership**
- Day 29: Leadership as Service
- Day 30: Leading with Integrity
- Day 31: Humility in Leadership
- Day 32: Leading with Vision and Compassion
- Day 33: Accountability and Growth
- Day 34: Raising Other Leaders
- Day 35: Leading Through Challenges
- Mentor Moment — Week 5
- Deborah Activation Journal — Week 5

Week 6 — Trusting God's Timing
- Day 36: The Seasons of Preparation
- Day 37: Delayed but Not Denied
- Day 38: Learning to Rest
- Day 39: When Doors Close
- Day 40: Divine Acceleration
- Day 41: Patience in Leadership
- Day 42: Appointed Time
- Mentor Moment — Week 6
- Deborah Activation Journal — Week 6

Week 7 — Spiritual Warfare & Mindset Mastery
- Day 43: Strength in the Spirit
- Day 44: Guarding Your Mind
- Day 45: Standing on the Word
- Day 46: Discerning the Real Battle
- Day 47: Mindset of Victory
- Day 48: The Power of Prayer and Fasting
- Day 49: Peace as a Weapon
- Mentor Moment — Week 7
- Deborah Activation Journal — Week 7

PART III — ARISE AND BUILD

Week 8 — Walking in Victory
- Day 50: Living from Victory, Not for It
- Day 51: Gratitude as a Strategy
- Day 52: The Power of Joy
- Day 53: Testimony and Influence
- Day 54: Maintaining Momentum
- Day 55: Protecting What You've Built
- Day 56: Celebration and Rest
- Mentor Moment — Week 8
- Deborah Activation Journal — Week 8

Week 9 — Legacy & Multiplication
- Day 57: The Call to Legacy
- Day 58: Multiplying Impact
- Day 59: Leaving a Kingdom Mark
- Day 60: The Leader's Commission
- Mentor Moment — Week 9
- Deborah Activation Journal — Week 9

CLOSING

Arise Leadership Declaration
Commissioning Prayer
Share Your Testimony
Continue the Journey
Next 30 Days Action Plan
After the 60 Days — Reflection Pages

WEEK 1
Answering the Call

DAY 1: YOU ARE CALLED

Scripture:

"But you are not like that, for you are a chosen people. You are royal priests, a holy nation, God's very own possession." — 1 Peter 2:9 (NLT)

Reflection:

Before Deborah led a nation, she first carried an identity. God did not call her because she was perfect, He called her because she was willing, positioned and aligned.

Your calling begins long before your assignment becomes visible. It starts with God's declaration over your life.

You are not an afterthought.

You are not a mistake.

You are not behind.

You are called: intentionally, specifically and purposefully - for this generation.

The enemy fights calling early because he knows identity shapes destiny. When you accept who God says you are, confidence rises, clarity strengthens and hesitation loses its grip.

Deborah did not wake up one day and decide to lead Israel, God called her and she responded.

Today begins your response.

Prayer:

Lord, anchor me in the truth of who I am in You. Silence every lie that challenges my identity and awaken a deep conviction that I am called according to Your purpose. Amen.

Action Step:

Write a personal "I am called" statement. Use Scripture or your own words. Read it aloud three times today as a declaration of identity.

(Use the following page for journaling and reflection.)

DAY 1: YOU ARE CALLED

Journaling Space:

DAY 2: CHOSEN FOR A PURPOSE

Scripture:

"For we are God's masterpiece. He has created us anew in Christ Jesus, so we can do the good things He planned for us long ago." — Ephesians 2:10 (NLT)

Reflection:

You were not just called — you were chosen, crafted, and positioned with purpose. God does nothing randomly. Before you took your first breath, God designed a path for you that carries impact, influence, and divine intention.

Deborah understood that her leadership was not about her — it was about the assignment God placed in her hands. Purpose is never accidental; it is always strategic. Your gifts, personality, experiences, and even the battles you've survived are part of your preparation.

Purpose is not something you "find."

Purpose is something you accept.

It is already within you, waiting to be activated.

As you embark on this 60-day journey, remind yourself that God chose you with intention. You are here because Heaven has a plan for your voice, your leadership, your business, your family, and your legacy.

Prayer:

Father, thank You for choosing me with purpose and intention. Reveal the assignments You have prepared for me, and help me walk boldly in them with clarity and confidence. Amen.

Action Step:

List three areas of your life where you sense purpose stirring. Pray over each one, asking God to show you how He intends to use you there.

(Use the following page for journaling and reflection.)

DAY 2: CHOSEN FOR A PURPOSE

Journaling Space:

DAY 3: OVERCOMING FEAR

Scripture:

"For God has not given us a spirit of fear and timidity, but of power, love, and self-discipline." — 2 Timothy 1:7 (NLT)

Reflection:

Fear delays obedience and limits potential. Deborah trusted the Caller more than the conflict. You cannot follow fear and fulfill purpose at the same time. Courage begins as a decision: God is bigger than what threatens me.

Prayer:

Lord, where fear has silenced me, fill me with Your power, love, and a sound mind. Amen.

Action Step:

Name one area where fear has led. Write and speak a truth-declaration over it today.

Journaling Space:

DAY 3: OVERCOMING FEAR

Journaling Space:

DAY 4: WALKING BY FAITH

Scripture:

"For we live by believing and not by seeing." — 2 Corinthians 5:7 (NLT)

Reflection:

Faith acts before it fully understands. Deborah obeyed and watched victory unfold. Faith is not the absence of uncertainty; it is trust in motion—choosing God's unseen hand over visible circumstances.

Prayer:

Father, teach me to walk by faith when sight is limited. Steady me in Your timing and guidance. Amen.

Action Step:

Take one imperfect step of faith in an area you've stalled, waiting for ideal conditions.

Journaling Space:

DAY 4: WALKING BY FAITH

Journaling Space:

DAY 5: A WILLING HEART

Scripture:

"If you are willing and obedient, you will eat the good things of the land."
— Isaiah 1:19 (NLT)

Reflection:

Perfection isn't the requirement—willingness is. Deborah's strength was her ready "yes." Willingness opens the door to divine partnership; it's the soil where miracles take root.

Prayer:

Lord, shape my instincts toward obedience. Let my "yes" be ready before I see the outcome. Amen.

Action Step:

Pray: "God, whatever You ask, my answer is yes." Choose one area to practice obedience this week.

Journaling Space:

DAY 5: A WILLING HEART

Journaling Space:

DAY 6: STRENGTH FOR THE JOURNEY

Scripture:

"The Lord is my strength and my shield; my heart trusts in Him, and He helps me." — Psalm 28:7 (NLT)

Reflection:

Purpose is not sustained by willpower but by God's strength. Deborah didn't carry her assignment alone. When your energy empties, His remains. The One who called you will also carry you.

Prayer:

Father, be my strength and my shield. Renew me so I can complete what You've entrusted. Amen.

Action Step:

Pause for ten minutes to invite God's presence. Journal how His strength feels different from striving.

Journaling Space:

DAY 6: STRENGTH FOR THE JOURNEY

Journaling Space:

DAY 7: PREPARING FOR THE NEXT STEP

Scripture:

"Commit your actions to the Lord, and your plans will succeed."
— Proverbs 16:3 (NLT)

Reflection:

Preparation is a form of faith. Deborah planned with prayer and moved with purpose. God defines success by surrender, not speed. Commit your work to Him and let alignment lead to acceleration.

Prayer:

Lord, I commit my plans to You. Order my steps and align my preparation with Your purpose. Amen.

Action Step:

List three practical ways to prepare for what God is calling you to do; start one this week.

Journaling Space:

DAY 7: PREPARING FOR THE NEXT STEP

Journaling Space:

MENTOR MOMENT — WEEK 1

Theme: Identity & Calling

Before you can arise as a Deborah, you must first settle who you are. Identity is the foundation of influence, purpose and spiritual authority. Too many women try to lead without first establishing who they are in God. Deborah's strength did not come from title, it came from identity. She knew who called her and that clarity shaped every decision she made.

This week, ground yourself in truth. Let God redefine what life may have mislabeled. Identity is not shaped by experience, success, or failure, it is anchored in revelation. When you know who you are, you stop shrinking, apologizing and second-guessing what God placed within you. Identity produces stability. Stability produces confidence. Confidence produces movement.

Your calling is not fragile and neither are you. Build your life on the unshakable truth of who God says you are, and every room you enter will adjust accordingly.

DEBORAH ACTIVATION JOURNAL — WEEK 1

Theme: Hearing and Responding to God's Invitation to Rise

Heart Alignment

- What did God call you toward this week?

- Where did you resist, and what would obedience look like next time?

Leadership in Motion

- How did you lead yourself/others in faith?

- What did you learn about your influence or your fears?

Business & Strategy Activation

- Identify one area of work/finance that requires realignment with purpose.

- What strategic step can you pray over and act on this week?

Kingdom in Motion Challenge

- Take one deliberate, public step of obedience (call, proposal, testimony, or mentoring conversation).

DEBORAH ACTIVATION JOURNAL — WEEK 1

Journaling Space:

WEEK 2
Courage in Leadership

DAY 8: THE CALL TO LEAD

Scripture:

"The Lord surely is with you, mighty warrior." — *Judges 6:12 (NLT)*

Reflection:

Leadership requires courage before competence. God often calls us into roles we do not feel ready for, not to expose our weaknesses but to reveal His strength. Deborah responded to God's call not because she felt powerful, but because she trusted the One who empowered her. When God speaks a calling over your life, whether in your home, workplace, ministry, or business, it is because He has already placed within you what is needed. Leadership begins with willingness.

Prayer:

Lord, give me the courage to step into the roles You have prepared for me. Help me to see myself through Your eyes and trust Your presence as my confidence. Amen.

Action Step:

Identify one area where you've been avoiding leadership. Take one practical step toward embracing that role this week.

Journaling Space:

DAY 8: THE CALL TO LEAD

Journaling Space:

DAY 9 – THE POWER OF OBEDIENCE

Scripture:

"So be strong and courageous! Do not be afraid or discouraged. For the Lord your God is with you wherever you go." — Joshua 1:9 (NLT)

Reflection:

Obedience is the foundation of courageous leadership. Deborah moved decisively because she trusted God's instruction more than her own hesitation. Obedience demands discipline—acting even when clarity is incomplete. When you obey quickly, you limit the room fear has to grow. God does not expect perfection in your steps, only willingness in your heart.

Prayer:

Father, give me a disciplined spirit that responds quickly to Your direction. Strengthen my commitment to obey even when the path is unclear. Amen.

Action Step:

Write down one instruction you sense God has given you but you've delayed acting on. Take a measurable step toward completing it today.

Journaling Space:

DAY 9 – THE POWER OF OBEDIENCE

Journaling Space:

DAY 10 – COURAGE IN CONFLICT

Scripture:

"The battle is the Lord's." — *1 Samuel 17:47 (NLT)*

Reflection:

Leadership attracts resistance. Deborah faced conflict because her leadership disrupted complacency and challenged the status quo. Courage is not the absence of difficulty; it is the ability to remain anchored despite it. When you understand that the battle belongs to God, you no longer internalize opposition—you interpret it correctly. God fights for those He assigns.

Prayer:

Lord, anchor my heart when I face conflict. Help me respond with wisdom and calm assurance that the battle belongs to You, not me. Amen.

Action Step:

Identify one conflict or tension in your life. Pray over it intentionally and determine a wise, measured next step.

Journaling Space:

DAY 10 – COURAGE IN CONFLICT

Journaling Space:

DAY 11 – SPEAKING WITH AUTHORITY

Scripture:

"The mouth of the righteous speaks wisdom, and his tongue speaks justice."
— Psalm 37:30 (NLT)

Reflection:

Authority is not loud; it is rooted in truth. Deborah spoke with clarity because her words aligned with God's direction. Your voice carries influence—not through force, but through alignment. Leadership demands truthful communication, righteous counsel, and words that bring clarity rather than confusion.

Prayer:

Holy Spirit, guide my words today. Let what I speak reflect Your wisdom, Your justice, and Your heart. Amen.

Action Step:

Consider one conversation, email, or decision where your voice is required. Speak truthfully and with confidence.

Journaling Space:

DAY 11 – SPEAKING WITH AUTHORITY

Journaling Space:

DAY 12 – LEADING WITH COMPASSION

Scripture:

"Clothe yourselves with tenderhearted mercy, kindness, humility, gentleness, and patience." — Colossians 3:12 (NLT)

Reflection:

Deborah shows us that leadership is both strength and softness. Authority without compassion becomes domination; compassion without conviction becomes indecision. The greatest leaders carry both. Leading with compassion does not weaken your effectiveness—it strengthens your impact. People follow leaders who see them, hear them, and value them.

Prayer:

Lord, form compassion in me. Help me lead in a way that uplifts, strengthens, and reflects Your heart. Amen.

Action Step:

Extend intentional kindness or support to someone you lead or influence today.

Journaling Space:

DAY 12 – LEADING WITH COMPASSION

Journaling Space:

DAY 13 – WISDOM IN DECISION-MAKING

Scripture:

"If you need wisdom, ask our generous God, and He will give it to you."
— James 1:5 (NLT)

Reflection:

Leadership requires decisions, and decisions require wisdom. Deborah listened before she acted. A wise leader consults God first, rather than navigating by urgency or emotion. Wisdom is not hesitation; it is clarity produced through seeking God's counsel.

Prayer:

God, grant me wisdom for the decisions I must make. Let peace confirm what is from You and confusion reveal what is not. Amen.

Action Step:

Before making a significant decision this week, pause. Pray. Journal what you sense God revealing.

Journaling Space:

DAY 13 – WISDOM IN DECISION-MAKING

Journaling Space:

DAY 14 – TRUSTING GOD'S TIMING

Scripture:

"For everything there is a season, a time for every activity under heaven."
— Ecclesiastes 3:1 (NLT)

Reflection:

Deborah understood divine timing. Leaders must know when to move and when to wait. Rushing leads to frustration; waiting with fear leads to stagnation. Trusting God's timing protects the vision He entrusted to you. When you align with His pace, you avoid unnecessary battles and wasted energy.

Prayer:

Lord, teach me to honor Your timing. Help me wait with faith, move with obedience, and remain aligned with Your plan. Amen.

Action Step:

List three areas where you feel impatient. Pray over each and release them into God's timing.

Journaling Space:

DAY 14 – TRUSTING GOD'S TIMING

Journaling Space:

MENTOR MOMENT — WEEK 2

Theme: Hearing God

Every Deborah leads from a place of spiritual clarity. The strength of your leadership is tied to the strength of your discernment. Hearing God is not a mystical experience, it is the fruit of alignment. When your mind is quiet, your spirit is attentive and your schedule makes room for Him, direction becomes clearer and decisions become simpler.

This week, lean into stillness. Leadership requires a listening ear. In business, in family, in ministry and in purpose every breakthrough will require strategy, and strategy flows from the presence of God. Deborah could direct a nation because she first sat under the palm tree to listen.

Protect your sensitivity to God's voice. The world will compete for your attention, but only one voice holds the wisdom, clarity, and timing that can change everything. Make hearing God your priority, not your last resort.

DEBORAH ACTIVATION JOURNAL — WEEK 2

Theme: Courage in Leadership

Heart Alignment

- Where did you feel God calling you into courage this week?
- What fears surfaced, and how did you address them?

Leadership in Motion

- Where did you lead with clarity or compassion?
- What leadership decisions stretched your faith?

Business & Strategy Activation

- Identify one decision requiring courage this week.
- What strategic step can you take with confidence?

Kingdom in Motion Challenge

- Take one courageous step: big or small that aligns with your calling this week.

DEBORAH ACTIVATION JOURNAL — WEEK 2

Journaling Space:

WEEK 3
Boldness in Action

DAY 15 – STEPPING FORWARD IN FAITH

Scripture:

"Faith shows the reality of what we hope for; it is the evidence of things we cannot see." — Hebrews 11:1 (NLT)

Reflection:

Faith always requires movement. It asks you to step even when the outcome is unclear. Deborah did not wait for perfect circumstances; she moved because God spoke. Boldness is not the absence of uncertainty — it is the decision to trust God beyond what you can calculate.

When God calls you forward, hesitation is often the first barrier. But every step of faith disrupts fear, strengthens courage, and opens doors that remain invisible until you move.

God is not asking you to see the whole picture — only to trust His leading.

Prayer:

Lord, give me the courage to step forward even when I cannot see the full path. Strengthen my trust in Your voice above all else. Amen.

Action Step:

Identify one step you have been delaying due to uncertainty. Take that step today — even if it's small.

Journaling Space:

DAY 15 – STEPPING FORWARD IN FAITH

Journaling Space:

DAY 16 – COURAGE TO OBEY

Scripture:

"Be strong and courageous! Do not be afraid or discouraged. For the Lord your God is with you wherever you go." — Joshua 1:9 (NLT)

Reflection:

Obedience requires courage. It asks you to align action with God's voice even when the direction feels stretching. Deborah's obedience positioned Israel for victory — her courage became the catalyst for breakthrough.

Courage is not a feeling; it is a conviction. It is the willingness to honor God with your decisions, your boundaries, your leadership, and your movement.

When you obey God courageously, Heaven backs your assignment.

Prayer:

Father, help me obey Your leading with boldness. Strengthen my heart to choose Your way even when it challenges my comfort. Amen.

Action Step:

Choose one area in your life that requires immediate obedience. Take one courageous step to honor God in that area today.

Journaling Space:

DAY 16 – COURAGE TO OBEY

Journaling Space:

DAY 17 – BREAKING THROUGH LIMITING BELIEFS

Scripture:

"For as he thinks in his heart, so is he." — Proverbs 23:7 (NKJV)

Reflection:

Your mindset determines your movement. Before you conquer anything outwardly, you must first conquer what limits you inwardly. Deborah did not shrink back because of her gender, role, or the culture of her time — she rose above limiting beliefs.

What limits your thinking limits your potential.

What limits your potential limits your purpose.

God wants to renew your mind so He can transform your life.

Prayer:

Lord, reveal every limiting belief that holds me back from my assignment. Replace each one with Your truth. Amen.

Action Step:

Write down three limiting beliefs that have shaped your decisions. Replace each one with a biblical truth.

Journaling Space:

DAY 17 – BREAKING THROUGH LIMITING BELIEFS

Journaling Space:

DAY 18 – BOLD DECLARATIONS

Scripture:

"Death and life are in the power of the tongue." — Proverbs 18:21 (NKJV)

Reflection:

What you speak shapes what you see. Deborah spoke with authority because she understood the power of her words. Bold declarations shift the atmosphere, build confidence, and anchor your spirit in truth.

Your voice carries weight in Heaven and on Earth. When you declare God's Word, you are aligning your present with His promise.

Prayer:

Father, purify my words. Teach me to speak life, strength, and purpose over myself and others. Amen.

Action Step:

Write three declarations that affirm your identity, purpose, and leadership. Speak them aloud today.

Journaling Space:

DAY 18 – BOLD DECLARATIONS

Journaling Space:

DAY 19 – FACING THE UNKNOWN

Scripture:

"When you pass through the waters, I will be with you." — *Isaiah 43:2 (NLT)*

Reflection:

Boldness is often revealed when God leads you into the unfamiliar. Deborah faced uncertainty — yet she trusted the God who went before her.

You may not know the details, but you know the God who holds every detail.

Courage is formed in seasons where clarity is limited but God's presence is certain.

Prayer:

Lord, walk with me into the places I do not yet understand. Let Your presence be my confidence. Amen.

Action Step:

Reflect on one area of uncertainty in your life. Pray specifically for God's presence, not just clarity.

Journaling Space:

DAY 19 – FACING THE UNKNOWN

Journaling Space:

DAY 20 – THE BOLDNESS TO START AGAIN

Scripture:

"The godly may trip seven times, but they will get up again."
— Proverbs 24:16 (NLT)

Reflection:

Boldness is not only needed to begin — it is needed to begin again. Failure is not final unless you stop rising. Deborah's journey reminds us that perseverance is a form of courage.

Every woman called by God must learn this truth:

Your setbacks do not cancel your calling.

Starting again is an act of spiritual warfare — it declares that purpose still lives within you.

Prayer:

Lord, give me the courage to rise again in the places where I've fallen or grown discouraged. Restore my strength and resolve. Amen.

Action Step:

Choose one area where you will "start again" today — spiritually, practically, or emotionally.

Journaling Space:

DAY 20 – THE BOLDNESS TO START AGAIN

Journaling Space:

DAY 21 – FAITH MADE VISIBLE

Scripture:

"So you see, faith by itself isn't enough. Unless it produces good deeds, it is dead and useless." — James 2:17 (NLT)

Reflection:

Faith is not hidden; it is revealed through action. Deborah's faith produced movement — and movement produced victory.

Faith becomes powerful when it becomes visible.

Every step you take in obedience is evidence of your trust in God.

Your faith is not meant to stay in your journal. It is meant to show up in your decisions, habits, leadership, business, and relationships.

Prayer:

Father, let my faith be seen in my actions. Teach me to live out what I believe with boldness and conviction. Amen.

Action Step:

Identify one area where your actions need to match your faith. Take a visible step today.

Journaling Space:

DAY 21 – FAITH MADE VISIBLE

Journaling Space:

MENTOR MOMENT — WEEK 3

Theme: Courage & Obedience

Courage is not the absence of fear — it is the decision to move anyway. Every Deborah moment in Scripture required boldness: boldness to speak, boldness to lead, boldness to obey. You cannot walk in divine purpose while negotiating with fear.

This week confronted your obedience. Purpose will always demand movement, and fear will always suggest procrastination. But obedience is the proof that you trust God more than your comfort. Courage does not mean you feel ready — it means you respond when God says "go."

Do not wait for certainty to obey. Many doors will only open on the other side of obedience. Move when He speaks, and you will watch courage rise in places where fear once lived.

DEBORAH ACTIVATION JOURNAL — WEEK 3

Theme: Boldness in Action

Heart Alignment

- Where did God invite you to take bold action this week?

- In which moments did you hesitate, and why?

Leadership in Motion

- How did you step forward in faith, even when you felt unsure?

- What did you notice about how others responded to your obedience?

Business & Strategy Activation

- Identify one area (business, finances, ministry, or career) that requires a bold move.

- What is the next courageous, practical step you can take in that area?

Kingdom in Motion Challenge

- Do one thing this week that scares you a little but clearly aligns with your God-given assignment.

DEBORAH ACTIVATION JOURNAL — WEEK 3

Journaling Space:

WEEK 4

Wisdom and Strategy

DAY 22 – THE WISDOM TO WAIT AND LISTEN

Scripture:

"Be still, and know that I am God." — Psalm 46:10 (NLT)

Reflection:

Wisdom often begins with stillness. Deborah led with precision because she listened before she moved. God's strategy is rarely revealed in noise; it is uncovered in quiet obedience.

Waiting is not passive — it is strategic.

Listening is not inactivity — it is alignment.

God will give you the clarity you seek when you create space for His voice.

Prayer:

Lord, teach me to wait on You without anxiety and to listen without distraction. Align my heart with Your wisdom. Amen.

Action Step:

Spend five uninterrupted minutes in silence before God. Write what you sense Him whispering.

Journaling Space:

DAY 22 – THE WISDOM TO WAIT AND LISTEN

Journaling Space:

DAY 23 – DIVINE STRATEGY

Scripture:

"If any of you lacks wisdom, let him ask of God… and it will be given to him."
— James 1:5 (NKJV)

Reflection:

God does not expect you to lead without strategy. Deborah's wisdom did not come from self-reliance — it came from divine instruction. When God calls, He also equips.

You do not have to figure everything out alone. Wisdom is available to those who ask.

Every strategic insight you receive is a partnership with Heaven.

Prayer:

Father, grant me divine wisdom for every decision before me. Lead me in strategy that aligns with Your will. Amen.

Action Step:

Write down a decision you are currently facing. Ask God specifically for wisdom and wait for His guidance.

Journaling Space:

DAY 23 – DIVINE STRATEGY

Journaling Space:

DAY 24 – STEWARDING YOUR ASSIGNMENT

Scripture:

"Now it is required that those who have been given a trust must prove faithful."
— 1 Corinthians 4:2 (NIV)

Reflection:

Stewardship is an act of honour. Deborah stewarded her role with excellence, not because of recognition but because of conviction.

God blesses the woman who treats her assignment with care. Purpose requires intentionality, not negligence.

Excellence is worship.

Stewardship is obedience.

Faithfulness is leadership.

Prayer:

Lord, help me steward every assignment with integrity and excellence. Strengthen my hands to build what You have entrusted to me. Amen.

Action Step:

Choose one area (home, business, ministry, finances) to steward with greater intentionality this week.

Journaling Space:

DAY 24 – STEWARDING YOUR ASSIGNMENT

Journaling Space:

DAY 25 – DISCERNMENT IN DECISION-MAKING

Scripture:

"Trust in the Lord with all your heart; do not depend on your own understanding." — Proverbs 3:5 (NLT)

Reflection:

Not every open door is from God, and not every opportunity is aligned with purpose. Deborah led with discernment — she separated noise from instruction.

Discernment protects you from distractions, detours, and drainers.

It keeps your "yes" sacred and your "no" powerful.

Decisions made in God's wisdom led to peace, clarity, and fruitfulness.

Prayer:

Father, sharpen my discernment. Help me recognize Your voice in every decision. Close the doors that distract me and open the ones aligned with my purpose. Amen.

Action Step:

Review one major decision currently in front of you. Pray for discernment — then document the clarity you receive.

Journaling Space:

DAY 25 – DISCERNMENT IN DECISION-MAKING

Journaling Space:

DAY 26 – ORDER AND STRUCTURE

Scripture:

"For God is not a God of disorder but of peace." — *1 Corinthians 14:33 (NLT)*

Reflection:

Order is spiritual. Structure is protective. Systems create room for purpose to flow without chaos.

Deborah's leadership was strong because it was structured. She held court, offered judgment and created stability for a nation.

When your life is in order, clarity increases and stress decreases.

Prayer:

Lord, bring divine order to every area of my life. Help me build rhythms that support my purpose and leadership. Amen.

Action Step:

Choose one area (schedule, workspace, finances, routines) to bring into order. Implement one practical system today.

Journaling Space:

DAY 26 – ORDER AND STRUCTURE

Journaling Space:

DAY 27 – EXCELLENCE AS WORSHIP

Scripture:

"And whatever you do, do it heartily, as to the Lord..." — Colossians 3:23 (NKJV)

Reflection:

Excellence is not perfection — it is devotion. It is doing your best as an offering to God.

Deborah led with excellence because she understood that her work represented God's character through her leadership.

Your attitude, your diligence, and your commitment speak louder than your words.

Let excellence become the standard of your life — not to impress others but to honor God.

Prayer:

Lord, help me approach every task with excellence. Let my work reveal Your character and bring glory to Your name. Amen.

Action Step:

Choose one task today to complete with intentional, God-honoring excellence.

Journaling Space:

DAY 27 – EXCELLENCE AS WORSHIP

Journaling Space:

DAY 28 – STRATEGIC PREPARATION

Scripture:

"Commit your actions to the Lord, and your plans will succeed."
— Proverbs 16:3 (NLT)

Reflection:

Preparation is a form of faith. Deborah did not wait for crisis to seek God; she prepared consistently.

Preparedness increases capacity, reduces anxiety, and positions you for success.

When you prepare strategically, you honor God with your diligence.

Prayer:

Father, align my preparation with Your purpose. Help me plan with wisdom, discipline, and spiritual clarity. Amen.

Action Step:

Take one goal and break it into three actionable steps. Begin the first step today.

Journaling Space:

DAY 28 – STRATEGIC PREPARATION

Journaling Space:

MENTOR MOMENT — WEEK 4

Theme: Stewardship & Discipline

Every Deborah carries responsibility. Purpose requires structure, discipline, and wise stewardship. What God gives must be managed intentionally, your time, your finances, your relationships and your assignments.

This week challenged you to examine your habits, your order, and your commitment. Discipline is not punishment; it is preparation. It makes you trustworthy with more. Deborah ruled a nation because she stewarded her role with excellence and consistency.

Evaluate where you are growing and where you are drifting. Realignment is not failure, it is wisdom. When your life is in order, purpose flows with ease. When your habits support your calling, you become unstoppable.

DEBORAH ACTIVATION JOURNAL — WEEK 4

Theme: Wisdom & Strategy

Heart Alignment

- What did God reveal to you about your current habits and patterns?

- Where do you sense Him inviting you into greater order or discipline?

Leadership in Motion

- How did you apply wisdom in your decisions this week?

- Where did strategy help you avoid confusion, delay, or burnout?

Business & Strategy Activation

- Identify one area (calendar, money, systems, relationships) that needs clearer structure.

- What is one strategic shift you can implement in the next 7 days?

Kingdom in Motion Challenge

- Create or refine one practical system (planner, budget, routine, workflow) that will support your purpose long-term.

DEBORAH ACTIVATION
JOURNAL — WEEK 4

Journaling Space:

WEEK 5
Godly Leadership

DAY 29 – LEADERSHIP AS SERVICE

Scripture:

"The greatest among you must be a servant." — Matthew 23:11 (NLT)

Reflection:

In the Kingdom, leadership is not a position of privilege but of service. Deborah led by lifting others, her influence empowered Barak and encouraged a nation. True authority is proven in humility.

The higher you rise, the lower you must bow. Servant leadership is the foundation that sustains divine promotion.

Prayer:

Lord, teach me to lead through service. Help me to honour people, listen with compassion and influence with integrity. Amen.

Action Step:

Look for one opportunity today to serve someone you lead. Let your action speak louder than your title.

Journaling Space:

DAY 29 – LEADERSHIP AS SERVICE

Journaling Space:

DAY 30 – LEADING WITH INTEGRITY

Scripture:

"People with integrity walk safely, but those who follow crooked paths will slip and fall." — Proverbs 10:9 (NLT)

Reflection:

Integrity is leadership's greatest currency. Deborah's authority endured because her character was consistent. God promotes those who can be trusted in private as much as in public.

Integrity is not perfection, it is alignment between what you profess and what you practice.

Prayer:

Father, make me a leader of integrity. Purify my motives and help me make decisions that honour You, even when unseen. Amen.

Action Step:

Review one recent decision. Was it made from integrity or convenience? If needed, make it right.

Journaling Space:

DAY 30 – LEADING WITH INTEGRITY

Journaling Space:

DAY 31 – HUMILITY IN LEADERSHIP

Scripture:

"God opposes the proud but gives grace to the humble." — James 4:6 (NLT)

Reflection:

Deborah carried power without pride. Humility doesn't diminish authority, it multiplies it. The humble heart becomes a vessel through which God's grace flows freely.

Arrogance seeks credit; humility seeks impact. True leaders give glory to God and lift others higher.

Prayer:

Lord, keep my heart humble as You elevate my influence. May my leadership reflect Your grace, not my ego. Amen.

Action Step:

Affirm someone else's contribution today. Acknowledge publicly or privately how their efforts add value.

Journaling Space:

DAY 31 – HUMILITY IN LEADERSHIP

Journaling Space:

DAY 32 – LEADING WITH VISION AND COMPASSION

Scripture:

"Without vision the people perish." — Proverbs 29:18 (NLT)

Reflection:

Vision gives direction; compassion gives connection. Deborah's leadership combined both—she saw the future clearly while caring for her people deeply. A leader who only drives outcomes without empathy loses trust.

Effective leadership demands both head and heart.

Prayer:

God, help me to lead with balance—clarity in vision and compassion in execution. Amen.

Action Step:

Review your team, family, or circle of influence. Identify one person who needs encouragement or clarity of vision this week and reach out.

Journaling Space:

DAY 32 – LEADING WITH VISION AND COMPASSION

Journaling Space:

DAY 33 – ACCOUNTABILITY AND GROWTH

Scripture:

"The wise listen to advice and accept discipline, and at the end they will be counted among the wise." — Proverbs 19:20 (NLT)

Reflection:

Leadership without accountability becomes arrogance. Deborah sought counsel and stayed teachable. Correction doesn't weaken a leader; it strengthens her capacity.

Growth happens when feedback is embraced, not avoided.

Prayer:

Lord, make me a teachable leader. Surround me with people who challenge and refine me in love. Amen.

Action Step:

Invite feedback from someone you trust about how you lead or communicate. Receive it with humility and gratitude.

Journaling Space:

DAY 33 – ACCOUNTABILITY AND GROWTH

Journaling Space:

DAY 34 – RAISING OTHER LEADERS

Scripture:

"What you have heard from me... teach these truths to other trustworthy people who will be able to pass them on to others." — 2 Timothy 2:2 (NLT)

Reflection:

Godly leaders multiply themselves. Deborah's courage inspired other leaders, proving that leadership is legacy. The true test of influence is not what you achieve alone but who rises because of you.

Raising others requires generosity of time, wisdom and patience but it ensures Kingdom continuity.

Prayer:

Father, help me to invest in others as You've invested in me. Show me who to mentor, guide, or equip in this season. Amen.

Action Step:

Identify one emerging leader in your life. Reach out to encourage or mentor her intentionally this week.

Journaling Space:

DAY 34 – RAISING OTHER LEADERS

Journaling Space:

DAY 35 – LEADING THROUGH CHALLENGES

Scripture:

"When you go through deep waters, I will be with you." — Isaiah 43:2 (NLT)

Reflection:

Leadership will test your resilience. Deborah faced seasons of uncertainty yet remained steady because her confidence rested in God, not in outcomes. Challenges refine leaders—they expose weakness and reveal dependence on divine strength.

When you lead through difficulty, others learn faith through your endurance.

Prayer:

God, sustain me through every challenge. Remind me that Your presence is constant, even when the path is unclear. Amen.

Action Step:

Journal one current challenge and how you've seen God's hand in it so far. End with a declaration of faith over that situation.

Journaling Space:

DAY 35 – LEADING THROUGH CHALLENGES

Journaling Space:

MENTOR MOMENT — WEEK 5

Theme: Godly Leadership

Leadership is not about position; it is about posture. Godly leadership is shaped by humility, integrity, and the courage to serve. Deborah influenced a nation because she led with character, not ego.

This week revealed that leadership is not glamorous, it is sacrificial. It requires emotional maturity, spiritual strength and a willingness to put mission above comfort. To lead well, you must master yourself before you can guide others.

Remember this: authority is given but influence is earned. The people around you are shaped by the consistency you model, the words you speak and the decisions you make. Lead from a place of conviction and compassion, and your legacy will outlive you.

DEBORAH ACTIVATION JOURNAL — WEEK 5

Theme: Godly Leadership

Heart Alignment

- How did God challenge your motives and mindset this week?
- Where did humility create unexpected strength?

Leadership in Motion

- Which decisions or actions reflected servant leadership?
- How are you currently empowering or uplifting others?

Business & Strategy Activation

- Identify one area where integrity, structure, or communication needs to be strengthened.
- What concrete adjustment will you make to lead better in that area?

Kingdom in Motion Challenge

- Intentionally mentor, encourage, or uplift one woman this week in her calling.

DEBORAH ACTIVATION JOURNAL — WEEK 5

Journaling Space:

WEEK 6
Trusting God's Timing

DAY 36 – THE SEASONS OF PREPARATION

Scripture:

"For everything there is a season, a time for every activity under heaven."
— Ecclesiastes 3:1 (NLT)

Reflection:

Every purpose unfolds in seasons. Deborah's leadership didn't begin in public, it began in preparation. Hidden seasons are not punishment; they are the training grounds for endurance, character, and wisdom.

God uses preparation to strengthen what He plans to reveal. When you embrace your current season, you honour His process.

Prayer:

Lord, help me to see this season through Your eyes. Teach me to trust that what You're building in secret will one day bear fruit in public. Amen.

Action Step:

Write down what this current season has taught you about patience and purpose.

Journaling Space:

DAY 36 – THE SEASONS OF PREPARATION

Journaling Space:

DAY 37 – DELAYED BUT NOT DENIED

Scripture:

"The vision is for a future time... Though it tarries, wait for it; it will surely take place." — Habakkuk 2:3 (NLT)

Reflection:

Delays do not mean denial. Many abandon their assignment because the timing didn't match expectations. Deborah trusted God's pace even when outcomes weren't immediate.

Divine delay refines motives and proves readiness. If it's from God, delay cannot destroy it, it only matures it.

Prayer:

Father, give me patience to trust Your divine timing. Help me to see waiting not as wasted time but as preparation for promise. Amen.

Action Step:

Revisit one goal or prayer you've shelved out of discouragement. Ask God if the timing has shifted or if He's still preparing you for it.

Journaling Space:

DAY 37 – DELAYED BUT NOT DENIED

Journaling Space:

DAY 38 – LEARNING TO REST

Scripture:

"Come to me, all of you who are weary and carry heavy burdens, and I will give you rest." — Matthew 11:28 (NLT)

Reflection:

Rest is not inactivity—it's trust in motion. Deborah's leadership was effective because it was anchored in rhythm: hearing, acting, then resting. Rest renews discernment and protects from burnout.

Rest is a declaration of dependence on God's strength over your own.

Prayer:

Lord, teach me to rest in Your presence. Help me to release anxiety and trust that You're working while I wait. Amen.

Action Step:

Take one intentional break today—no devices, no tasks, only quiet gratitude. Reflect on what peace feels like in your body and spirit.

Journaling Space:

DAY 38 - LEARNING TO REST

Journaling Space:

DAY 39 - WHEN DOORS CLOSE

Scripture:

"We can make our plans, but the Lord determines our steps."
— Proverbs 16:9 (NLT)

Reflection:

Closed doors can be divine protection. Deborah's discernment allowed her to know when to move forward and when to pause. Some opportunities are good, but not God ordained.

A closed door doesn't mean failure, it means direction. God closes what could compromise your calling.

Prayer:

God, help me to trust you in every redirection. Give me wisdom to see closed doors as protection, not rejection. Amen.

Action Step:

Reflect on one door that closed recently. Write how that experience might actually be God's mercy, guiding you to better alignment.

Journaling Space:

DAY 39 – WHEN DOORS CLOSE

Journaling Space:

DAY 40 – DIVINE ACCELERATION

Scripture:

"At the right time, I, the Lord, will make it happen." — Isaiah 60:22 (NLT)

Reflection:

When the appointed time comes, what once seemed delayed will unfold quickly. Deborah waited for God's timing and when the moment arrived, victory came suddenly.

Acceleration is God redeeming time once surrendered to His process.

Prayer:

Lord, I trust that You will bring everything together in Your perfect timing. Prepare me to handle acceleration with humility and stewardship. Amen.

Action Step:

Write down one promise you're waiting on. Declare that God's timing—not human effort—will bring it to pass.

Journaling Space:

DAY 40 – DIVINE ACCELERATION

Journaling Space:

DAY 41 – PATIENCE IN LEADERSHIP

Scripture:

"We do not want you to become lazy but to imitate those who through faith and patience inherit what has been promised." — Hebrews 6:12 (NLT)

Reflection:

Leadership demands patience. Deborah's endurance inspired others because she never led from impulse. True leaders know how to wait well: working, praying and preparing while trusting the unseen.

Impatience births mistakes; patience births maturity.

Prayer:

God, develop in me a patient heart that leads with calm wisdom. Let my example teach others to trust You fully. Amen.

Action Step:

Notice how you respond when progress feels slow. Write what patience could look like in your actions this week.

Journaling Space:

DAY 41 – PATIENCE IN LEADERSHIP

Journaling Space:

DAY 42 – APPOINTED TIME

Scripture:

"He has made everything beautiful in its time." — Ecclesiastes 3:11 (NLT)

Reflection:

When the time is right, God makes all things align perfectly. Deborah's story reminds us that purpose is never late, it's perfectly timed.

When you trust His calendar, you free yourself from comparison. What God ordains for you will not miss you.

Prayer:

Father, I surrender my timeline to You. Teach me to trust that every season has meaning and every delay has purpose. Amen.

Action Step:

Reflect on the most significant season in your life so far. What did it teach you about God's faithfulness and timing?

Journaling Space:

DAY 42 – APPOINTED TIME

Journaling Space:

MENTOR MOMENT — WEEK 6

Theme: Trusting God's Timing

Purpose unfolds in seasons. Rushing leads to regret; waiting leads to wisdom. Deborah did not force timing, she aligned with it.

This week taught you patience, surrender, and trust. God's timing is never late, never early, and always strategic. The waiting room is not punishment, it is refinement. God is developing capacity, healing, clarity, and maturity.

Stop rushing the chapters God has not written yet. You are not behind; you are being prepared. The same God who called you will position you. The promise has an appointed time and when it arrives, it will not be delayed.

DEBORAH ACTIVATION JOURNAL — WEEK 6

Theme: Trusting God's Timing

Heart Alignment

- What did God reveal to you about timing this week?
- Where did you see His protection in doors that were delayed or closed?

Leadership in Motion

- How did patience shape your responses and decisions?
- What did surrender teach you about control and trust?

Business & Strategy Activation

- Identify one area where you've been rushing or striving.
- How can you slow down, seek God, and lead with clarity instead?

Kingdom in Motion Challenge

- Choose one goal or project and intentionally pause frantic striving. Pray specifically for alignment, not just acceleration.

DEBORAH ACTIVATION JOURNAL — WEEK 6

Journaling Space:

WEEK 7
Spiritual Warfare and Mindset Mastery

DAY 43 – STRENGTH IN THE SPIRIT

Scripture:

"Be strong in the Lord and in His mighty power." — Ephesians 6:10 (NLT)

Reflection:

Deborah's strength came from the Spirit of God, not personal willpower. Leadership without spiritual strength collapses under pressure. You are not asked to fight alone; Heaven fights with you.

When your confidence comes from communion with God, no opposition can dislodge you. Victory begins in the spirit before it appears in the natural.

Prayer:

Lord, fill me with your Spirit today. Let every battle I face remind me that your power is greater than my fear. Amen.

Action Step:

Spend time praying in silence or worship, intentionally drawing on God's strength for today's challenges.

Journaling Space:

DAY 43 – STRENGTH IN THE SPIRIT

Journaling Space:

DAY 44 – GUARDING YOUR MIND

Scripture:

"Do not be conformed to this world, but be transformed by the renewing of your mind." — Romans 12:2 (NLT)

Reflection:

The battleground of every leader is the mind. Before you lose ground externally, the enemy attacks your thoughts internally. Deborah guarded her perspective through the truth of God's Word.

Mind renewal is not occasional; it is daily discipline. Whatever fills your mind will eventually form your decisions.

Prayer:

Father, renew my mind with Your truth. Silence every thought that contradicts Your Word. Amen.

Action Step:

List three recurring negative thoughts. Beside each, write one Scripture that replaces it with truth.

Journaling Space:

DAY 44 – GUARDING YOUR MIND

Journaling Space:

DAY 45 – STANDING ON THE WORD

Scripture:

"Take the sword of the Spirit, which is the word of God." — Ephesians 6:17 (NLT)

Reflection:

God's Word is not only instruction—it is a weapon. Deborah's authority rested on divine promises. When you speak the Word, you shift atmospheres. Every lie must bow to truth spoken in faith.

Learn to fight spiritually, not emotionally. Victory belongs to those who declare God's Word with conviction.

Prayer:

Lord, teach me to use Your Word as my weapon. Let Scripture become my first response, not my last resort. Amen.

Action Step:

Memorize one verse that strengthens your faith in this season. Speak it aloud whenever doubt arises.

Journaling Space:

DAY 45 - STANDING ON THE WORD

Journaling Space:

DAY 46 – DISCERNING THE REAL BATTLE

Scripture:

"For we are not fighting against flesh-and-blood enemies, but against evil rulers and authorities of the unseen world." — Ephesians 6:12 (NLT)

Reflection:

Many battles that appear physical are actually spiritual. Deborah discerned beyond appearances; she fought the right enemy. Discernment keeps you from wasting energy on distractions.

Ask God daily, "What is the real battle here?" Clarity reveals strategy.

Prayer:

Holy Spirit, open my eyes to see what is truly happening around me. Help me fight with wisdom, not emotion. Amen.

Action Step:

Think of a current conflict. Ask God to show you what's beneath the surface—fear, pride, or spiritual opposition—and respond with prayer, not reaction.

Journaling Space:

DAY 46 – DISCERNING THE REAL BATTLE

Journaling Space:

DAY 47 – MINDSET OF VICTORY

Scripture:

"Thanks be to God, who gives us the victory through our Lord Jesus Christ."
— 1 Corinthians 15:57 (NLT)

Reflection:

Victory begins as a mindset before it manifests as an outcome. Deborah never doubted that God would deliver Israel because she trusted His Word more than her circumstances.

A victorious mindset is not denial of reality, it is devotion to truth.

Prayer:

Lord, renew my mindset for victory. Help me think as one who has already overcome through you. Amen.

Action Step:

Write three affirmations rooted in Scripture that declare your victory. Repeat them daily this week.

Journaling Space:

DAY 47 – MINDSET OF VICTORY

Journaling Space:

DAY 48 – THE POWER OF PRAYER AND FASTING

Scripture:

"This kind can be cast out only by prayer and fasting." — Mark 9:29 (NLT)

Reflection:

Some breakthroughs require deeper surrender. Deborah's discernment was sharpened through intimacy with God. Prayer aligns your heart; fasting clears your hearing. Together they unlock spiritual clarity and authority.

When you seek God in both prayer and discipline, the supernatural becomes natural.

Prayer:

Father, teach me to seek You with focus. Help me discipline my flesh so my spirit can hear You clearly. Amen.

Action Step:

Dedicate one meal or one hour this week to prayer and reflection instead of routine activity. Note any insights you receive.

Journaling Space:

DAY 48 – THE POWER OF PRAYER AND FASTING

Journaling Space:

DAY 49 – PEACE AS A WEAPON

Scripture:

"You will keep in perfect peace all who trust in You, all whose thoughts are fixed on You." — Isaiah 26:3 (NLT)

Reflection:

Peace is not passivity; it is power under control. Deborah ruled during chaos yet led from inner calm. Peace disarms the enemy because it shows unshakable trust in God.

Maintain peace and you maintain perspective. Where peace dwells, strategy flows.

Prayer:

Lord, make your peace my posture in every situation. Guard my heart and mind as I trust You completely. Amen.

Action Step:

When tension rises today, pause. Breathe deeply and silently pray: "I trust You, God." Record how your peace changed the outcome.

Journaling Space:

DAY 49 – PEACE AS A WEAPON

Journaling Space:

MENTOR MOMENT — WEEK 7

Theme: Spiritual Warfare & Mindset

You cannot lead spiritually with a defeated mind. Warfare often begins in thoughts long before it reaches circumstances. Deborah won because her mind was anchored, not tossed by fear, intimidation or confusion.

This week sharpened your awareness. Not every battle is natural; many are spiritual. The enemy fights location, purpose, identity, clarity and assignment. But your weapons: prayer, Scripture, peace, discernment are powerful and effective.

Master your mind and you master your momentum. Guard your thoughts, speak truth, reject lies and stand firm. Victory begins within before it manifests around you.

DEBORAH ACTIVATION JOURNAL — WEEK 7

Theme: Spiritual Warfare & Mindset Mastery

Heart Alignment

- Where did you experience spiritual resistance this week?

- What lies did God expose and replace with truth?

Leadership in Motion

- How did peace or discernment shape your decisions?

- Which spiritual discipline (prayer, worship, fasting, the Word) strengthened you most?

Business & Strategy Activation

- Identify one mindset shift needed to elevate your leadership, business, or ministry.

- What daily or weekly routine will help you guard your mental clarity?

Kingdom in Motion Challenge

- Dedicate one day this week to focused prayer or fasting for wisdom, protection, and clarity in your assignment.

DEBORAH ACTIVATION JOURNAL — WEEK 7

Journaling Space:

WEEK 8
Walking in Victory

DAY 50 – LIVING FROM VICTORY, NOT FOR IT

Scripture:

"But thank God! He gives us victory over sin and death through our Lord Jesus Christ." — 1 Corinthians 15:57 (NLT)

Reflection:

Deborah didn't fight to prove victory, she fought from a place of confidence in God's promise. You are not striving to earn success; you are stewarding what Heaven already secured.

When you live from victory, comparison and competition lose power. You begin to lead from rest, not pressure.

Prayer:

Lord, remind me that the outcome has already been written in Your favor. Help me live from assurance, not anxiety. Amen.

Action Step:

Reflect on one area where you've been striving. Shift your perspective and write what it means to operate from victory instead of for it.

Journaling Space:

DAY 50 – LIVING FROM VICTORY, NOT FOR IT

Journaling Space:

DAY 51 – GRATITUDE AS A STRATEGY

Scripture:

"Give thanks in all circumstances; for this is God's will for you who belong to Christ Jesus." — 1 Thessalonians 5:18 (NLT)

Reflection:

Gratitude is a mindset of victory. Deborah led with confidence because her heart was anchored in praise, not complaint. Gratitude realigns focus from what's missing to what's working.

When you thank God in advance, you train your mind to expect victory.

Prayer:

Father, cultivate gratitude in me. Teach me to praise You in the process, not just the outcome. Amen.

Action Step:

Write a gratitude list of five things God has done in the past month. Speak them aloud as a declaration of faith and thanksgiving.

Journaling Space:

DAY 51 – GRATITUDE AS A STRATEGY

Journaling Space:

DAY 52 – THE POWER OF JOY

Scripture:

"The joy of the Lord is your strength." — *Nehemiah 8:10 (NLT)*

Reflection:

Joy is spiritual fuel. It strengthens endurance and keeps your heart light under heavy responsibility. Deborah's joy came from the victory God gave His people, not from circumstance.

Joy is not denial; it is delight in divine assurance. Protect it fiercely.

Prayer:

Lord, restore my joy where it has dimmed. Let laughter and lightness return to my spirit as signs of Your strength within me. Amen.

Action Step:

Do one thing today that sparks joy: worship, dance, rest, or connect with someone who uplifts your faith and be intentional to uplift theirs as well.

Journaling Space:

DAY 52 – THE POWER OF JOY

Journaling Space:

DAY 53 – TESTIMONY AND INFLUENCE

Scripture:

"They have defeated him by the blood of the Lamb and by their testimony."
— *Revelation 12:11 (NLT)*

Reflection:

Your story carries power. Deborah's song after battle became a testimony that strengthened a nation. When you share what God has done, you turn experience into influence.

Testimony doesn't glorify you, it magnifies God. Your transparency becomes someone else's roadmap.

Prayer:

Lord, give me boldness to share my testimony. Use my story to encourage and liberate others. Amen.

Action Step:

Share one recent victory or lesson with a friend, family member, or online community. Be authentic and give glory to God.

Journaling Space:

DAY 53 – TESTIMONY AND INFLUENCE

Journaling Space:

DAY 54 – MAINTAINING MOMENTUM

Scripture:

"Let us run with endurance the race God has set before us."
— Hebrews 12:1 (NLT)

Reflection:

Victory requires maintenance. Deborah ensured that Israel's peace endured because she kept the people aligned with God's instruction. Winning once is good; sustaining victory is wisdom.

Momentum is built through daily devotion and disciplined stewardship. Don't coast, continue.

Prayer:

Father, help me sustain what You've started in me. Give me endurance to maintain spiritual and practical momentum. Amen.

Action Step:

Review one area of progress in your life. Identify two daily or weekly habits to keep that progress going.

Journaling Space:

DAY 54 - MAINTAINING MOMENTUM

Journaling Space:

DAY 55 – PROTECTING WHAT YOU'VE BUILT

Scripture:

"Guard your heart above all else, for it determines the course of your life."
— Proverbs 4:23 (NLT)

Reflection:

Victorious living requires vigilance. Deborah's discernment preserved the nation's peace for forty years. The same God who gave victory will give wisdom to protect it.

Guard your peace, your vision, and your values. Every victory requires boundaries.

Prayer:

God, help me to protect what You've entrusted to me. Keep my heart pure and my focus undistracted. Amen.

Action Step:

List three boundaries you need to strengthen: spiritual, relational or professional to preserve your peace. Commit to them for the road ahead.

Journaling Space:

DAY 55 – PROTECTING WHAT YOU'VE BUILT

Journaling Space:

DAY 56 – CELEBRATION AND REST

Scripture:

"The Lord has done great things for us, and we are filled with joy."
— *Psalm 126:3 (NLT)*

Reflection:

After victory, Deborah paused to celebrate. Celebration acknowledges God's faithfulness and resets your soul. Many move quickly to the next goal without gratitude for the last miracle.

Rest and rejoice; both are holy.

Prayer:

Lord, thank You for the victories of this season. Teach me to celebrate You in every success. Amen.

Action Step:

Plan one moment of celebration, alone or with others, to thank God for His work in your life.

Journaling Space:

DAY 56 – CELEBRATION AND REST

Journaling Space:

MENTOR MOMENT — WEEK 8

Theme: Walking in Victory

Victory is not an event, it is a lifestyle. Deborah did not experience a momentary triumph; she established peace for forty years. Sustained victory requires gratitude, discipline, stewardship and awareness.

This week shifted you from survival mode to victory posture. You learned that victory must be protected, celebrated and maintained. Momentum is preserved by the decisions you make after the breakthrough, not before it.

Walk with confidence. God has equipped you. You are no longer fighting battles you've already won. Stand tall. Move strategically. Live like a woman who knows the outcome has already been spoken over her.

DEBORAH ACTIVATION JOURNAL — WEEK 8

Theme: Walking in Victory

Heart Alignment

- Which victories — big or small — did you experience this week?
- How did gratitude shape your attitude and decisions?

Leadership in Motion

- How are you sustaining consistency and peace in this season?
- Who can you uplift, celebrate, or encourage from a place of victory?

Business & Strategy Activation

- What system, boundary, or habit is essential to preserve your long-term success?
- What needs refinement or reinforcement in the coming month?

Kingdom in Motion Challenge

- Share a testimony or word of encouragement with someone intentionally, pointing them to God's faithfulness.

DEBORAH ACTIVATION JOURNAL — WEEK 8

Journaling Space:

WEEK 9
Legacy and Multiplication

DAY 57 – THE CALL TO LEGACY

Scripture:

"Those who are wise will shine as bright as the sky, and those who lead many to righteousness will shine like the stars forever." — Daniel 12:3 (NLT)

Reflection:

Legacy is not built in a moment; it's forged through a lifetime of obedience. Deborah's influence didn't end with her victories, it echoed through generations.

Your obedience today becomes someone else's freedom tomorrow.

Legacy is leadership that outlives you.

Prayer:

Father, help me to build what Heaven remembers. Teach me to live beyond personal success and to lead in a way that multiplies righteousness. Amen.

Action Step:

List three values or lessons you want to pass on — to your family, team, or community.

Journaling Space:

DAY 57 - THE CALL TO LEGACY

Journaling Space:

DAY 58 – MULTIPLYING IMPACT

Scripture:

"The things you have heard … teach these truths to other trustworthy people who will be able to pass them on to others." — 2 Timothy 2:2 (NLT)

Reflection:

Multiplication is God's growth model. Deborah's wisdom didn't die with her, it spread through those she led.

Impact multiplies when you pour into others with intention. A Deborah doesn't hoard revelation; she reproduces it.

Investing in others is Kingdom expansion.

Prayer:

Lord, show me who I'm called to pour into. Help me equip others with wisdom, courage and clarity. Amen.

Action Step:

Identify one person or group you can mentor, teach or empower this quarter. Schedule a conversation or create a resource for them.

Journaling Space:

DAY 58 – MULTIPLYING IMPACT

Journaling Space:

DAY 59 – LEAVING A KINGDOM MARK

Scripture:

"Let your good deeds shine out for all to see, so that everyone will praise your heavenly Father." — Matthew 5:16 (NLT)

Reflection:

Legacy is not about fame; it's about fruit. Deborah's mark was justice, courage and faith that glorified God.

Your business, ministry, or leadership should leave evidence of divine excellence. When people encounter your work, they should encounter His heart.

Your influence is your offering.

Prayer:

God, let everything I build reflect You. May my excellence point others toward Your grace and truth. Amen.

Action Step:

Audit your current work: products, systems or relationships. Does it reflect Kingdom values? If not, refine it intentionally.

Journaling Space:

DAY 59 – LEAVING A KINGDOM MARK

Journaling Space:

DAY 60 – THE DEBORAH'S COMMISSION

Scripture:

"Arise, shine, for your light has come, and the glory of the Lord rises upon you."
— Isaiah 60:1 (NLT)

Reflection:

This is your commissioning. Deborah's story wasn't only about leadership; it was about alignment with divine destiny. You have been equipped, stretched and strengthened. Now it's time to walk in authority to build, to lead, to mentor and to multiply.

You are no longer waiting for permission. Heaven has already spoken: Arise.

Prayer:

Lord, I receive Your commission. Send me into every sphere You've assigned me to lead with wisdom, to love with courage and to multiply legacy. Amen.

Action Step:

Write your personal Deborah Declaration — a one-paragraph statement describing how you will lead, serve, and build from this day forward.

Journaling Space:

DAY 60 – THE DEBORAH'S COMMISSION

Journaling Space:

MENTOR MOMENT — WEEK 9

Theme: Legacy & Multiplication

Legacy is intentional. It is built through decisions, habits, values, and faithfulness. Deborah's impact shaped generations because she lived beyond herself.

This final week calls you to think generationally, not only about what you build but about who becomes better because you lived. Your leadership, faith, integrity and excellence are seeds that will grow long after your voice is silent.

The greatest mark you will ever make is the transformation you ignite in others. Multiply what God placed in you. Mentor. Teach. Build. Empower. Legacy is not what you leave behind, it is who rises because of you.

DEBORAH ACTIVATION JOURNAL — WEEK 9

Theme: Walking in Victory

Heart Alignment

- What does "legacy" mean to you now, after these 60 days?

- How has God shifted your understanding of success and impact?

Leadership in Motion

- Who are you intentionally raising, mentoring, or influencing?

- What rhythms or structures will help you multiply leadership in others?

Business & Strategy Activation

- What structural decisions (systems, documentation, delegation, automation) will preserve long-term stability and impact?

- Which area needs a clear succession, scaling, or multiplication plan?

Kingdom in Motion Challenge

- Write your Deborah Manifesto, a one-page statement outlining your commitments, values, and mission for the decade ahead.

DEBORAH ACTIVATION JOURNAL — WEEK 9

Journaling Space:

THE ARISE LEADERSHIP DECLARATION

Today, I arise with intention.

I step into the woman God designed me to be: courageous, wise, disciplined, and led by the Spirit.

I declare that I will walk in purpose and lead with integrity, humility, and strength.

I choose clarity over confusion, obedience over hesitation, faith over fear, and excellence over complacency.

I commit to seeking God's guidance before I make decisions, to steward my gifts faithfully, and to show up fully in every sphere He has entrusted to me in my home, my work, my relationships and my calling.

I will cultivate wisdom, practice discernment and honour my assignments with diligence.

Where God sends me, I will go.

What He speaks, I will follow.

What He places in my hands, I will build with devotion and strategy.

I declare that my leadership will be marked by compassion, boldness, and unshakeable faith.

I will rise in confidence, knowing that Heaven has equipped me, prepared me, and positioned me for such a time as this.

I arise:

to lead with purpose,

to serve with grace,

and to live a life that reflects God's light, love and glory.

> *"Arise, shine, for your light has come,*
> *and the glory of the Lord rises upon you."*
> *— Isaiah 60:1 (NLT)*

Signed on this day: _____

Name: _____

THE COMMISSIONING PRAYER

Father, in the name of Jesus,

I stand before You with a surrendered heart, ready to walk fully in the purpose You have written for my life. Today, I receive Your call with humility and courage.

I declare that I am aligned with Your will, anchored in Your Word, and strengthened by Your Spirit for every assignment ahead.

Lord, commission my steps.

Order my thoughts.

Purify my motives.

Sharpen my discernment.

And fill me with wisdom beyond my years and strength beyond my natural ability.

Clothe me with courage to obey You quickly and grace to lead with compassion, integrity, and excellence.

Let Your presence go before me, Your voice guide me, and Your power sustain me in every season.

Father, expand my influence for Your glory alone.

Use my life as a vessel of healing, justice, purpose, and truth.

Let everything I build reflect Your heart.

Let everything I touch carry Your anointing.

Let everything I say be spoken with Your wisdom.

I commit my gifts, my leadership, my calling, my family,

and my future into Your hands.

Strengthen me to stand firm, finish well, and multiply the impact You have entrusted to me.

As You did with Deborah, go before me, fight for me, speak through me, and raise me up to be a voice of righteousness, strategy and faith in my generation.

Today, I step forward commissioned by Heaven.

I arise with boldness.

I arise with clarity.

I arise with purpose.

In Jesus mighty name,

Amen.

TESTIMONY INVITATION PAGE

Share Your Journey

Your transformation matters.

Your breakthrough matters.

Your story has the power to unlock someone else's obedience.

If this devotional has impacted you — your faith, your purpose, your leadership, or your confidence — I invite you to share your testimony.

Your words may be the encouragement another woman needs to rise.

Share your story at:

www.financiallysavvygirl.com/testimony

Whether big or small, your testimony is part of the Deborah movement being awakened across the world.

Your voice builds legacy.

Your obedience multiplies impact.

THE DEBORAH'S CHARGE

THE DEBORAH'S CHARGE

As you complete this 60-day journey, remember:

this is not a conclusion — it is a commissioning.

You are stepping into a new dimension of clarity, courage, and spiritual authority.

The same Spirit that strengthened Deborah, the same wisdom that guided her decisions,

and the same boldness that empowered her leadership — rests upon you now.

You are called to build with excellence, lead with conviction, and carry God's presence into every room you enter.

Your obedience will shift atmospheres.

Your leadership will open doors for others.

Your faith will shape generations.

Walk with confidence.

Walk with discernment.

Walk with the unshakeable assurance that Heaven backs every step you take in purpose.

May your voice be rooted in truth,

your heart anchored in integrity,

and your decisions guided by divine wisdom.

This is your charge: Arise — and keep arising.

With strength and grace,

Aquilas K. Dapaah

Continue your journey at:
www.financiallysavvygirl.com

CONTINUE THE JOURNEY

This devotional may be complete, but your rise has only begun.

You are part of a generation of women called to lead with faith, wisdom, strategy, and courage.

My prayer is that what began on these pages will continue to shape your daily decisions,

your leadership, your relationships, your finances, and your walk with God.

To keep growing, learning, and building with purpose, stay connected:

Financially Savvy Girl

@financially_savvygirl

Inspiration, wealth wisdom, leadership elevation, and faith-filled encouragement.

Community: WINC — Women Investors Network Canada

@winc.investors

Community, mentorship, and wealth-building for women rising in leadership and financial purpose.

Resources: FSG Publishing

New books, devotionals, children's financial literacy resources, and tools for faith-driven living.

Visit www.financiallysavvygirl.com

for devotionals, books, courses, resources, and a community of women committed to purpose-driven leadership.

Keep arising.

Keep leading.

Keep multiplying what God placed in your hands.

The world is waiting for the woman you are becoming.

NEXT 30 DAYS ACTION PLAN

Your transformation deepens when revelation becomes rhythm.

Use this page to carry your momentum into the next month with intention and clarity.

1. SPIRITUAL FOCUS

What spiritual habit will you commit to daily or weekly?
(Prayer, Scripture, worship, fasting, quiet time...)

2. LEADERSHIP FOCUS

What leadership quality will you strengthen this month?
(Courage, humility, discipline, consistency...)

3. PURPOSE/ASSIGNMENT FOCUS

What project, calling, or responsibility requires your yes?

4. FINANCIAL/BUSINESS FOCUS

What strategy or stewardship shift do you need to implement?

5. RELATIONSHIP & COMMUNITY FOCUS

Who do you need to mentor, support, forgive, or reconnect with?

6. BOUNDARIES & WELLNESS

What boundary will help protect your peace and productivity?

7. ONE BIG STEP OF FAITH

What bold, courageous, God-aligned action will you take this month?

Keep this page visible. Review it weekly.

Move with intention. Lead with wisdom.

AFTER THE 60 DAYS — REFLECTION PAGES

After the 60 Days: Reflection & Renewal

Take time to reflect on your growth, your breakthroughs, and the shifts God has made in you.

This is where revelation becomes remembrance — and remembrance becomes strength.

Reflection Prompts

1. What has God revealed to me about my identity over the last 60 days?

2. What fears have I overcome or released?

3. What bold steps of faith did I take?

4. How has my leadership deepened or matured?

5. What habits, disciplines, or mindsets have changed?

6. What areas still need surrender, intentionality, or healing?

7. What is God inviting me into next?
(Assignments, shifts, relationships, new courage...)

8. My declaration moving forward:

www.ingramcontent.com/pod-product-compliance
Lightning Source LLC
Chambersburg PA
CBHW061148070526
44584CB00034B/4455